I dedicate this book to my two children, Layla Amerie and Jordan Royal, My Grandmother Phoebe, my Aunt Linda, and my favorite cousin Damian. All of who are my angels in Heaven.

I hope that I have made the five of you very proud. I will continue to strive for excellence. You are what is driving me.

I love each of you forever and always. We shall meet again one day in Heaven.

1

TABLE OF CONTENTS

DAY 26

STEP 5 TOWARDS MOVING FORWARD:

FOCUS ON THE POSITIVE

DAY 27

LET YOUR CHALLENGES ELEVATE YOU

DAY 28

MAKING A CONSCIENCE DECISION TO MOVE FORWARD

DAY 29

YOUR CHALLENGES CAN HELP OTHERS

DAY 30

SHARE YOUR TESTIMONY

GETTING TO KNOW JOURNEY SPEAKS

My name is Journey Speaks and I am originally from Chicago, Illinois. My family and I grew up in the suburban area called "Lincoln Park." I really enjoyed living there, because it was only about fifteen minutes away from the downtown area. It was a magnificent area to grow up in, because of the beautiful scenery, the diversity, and all of the adventurous things to do right in the area.

We relocated to Georgia more than fifteen years ago because of new opportunities, and it has been our home ever since. I attended college in Georgia and am currently doing what I love most, besides writing, working in the medical field. Working in the medical field provides me with the opportunity to work around an array of different people and to be a part of helping them also.

The secrets behind getting through the challenges in my life have been prayer, having faith in God, and trusting in Him with my whole heart. Sounds very simple and easy, but it has truly been a challenge indeed. I've learned to trust God when things are good and also to trust Him when things are bad. Even when things don't look possible, I find a way to trust in Him. I'm human, so at times I have to remind myself to not worry about things, and to give them to God. I've had to hand over my burdens to Him because they were way too heavy for me to carry around. It definitely took me awhile and a whole lot of practice to think on a level like that.

I created this book for you to use as a guide and resource. It is a 30-day challenge and a journey of understanding why we go through challenges and steps to take in order to move forward. After each day there are questions to reflect on and a section to journal your thoughts and whatever God speaks to you about.

I also share some of my personal experiences and how God helped me to overcome them. If I can make it through, you can too. Let me show you how.

I used to wonder why I was going through so many challenges in my life; especially at such a very young age. I was often confused and needed to get a better understanding of why these things were happening to me. Challenge after challenge was occurring in my life and it seemed as if I couldn't catch a break. One moment I was up, and the next, I was down. One minute it felt as if I was trapped in a cage. Then out of nowhere, I was released. It often felt as if I was on a roller coaster. Most of the challenges that I was going through were too much for me to bare - alone.

I know we are not supposed to question God, but I often wanted to for sure.
Sometimes I would look to God and wondered "why me"?

I knew I wasn't a bad person, so I wondered why was I going through so much?

What had I done so wrong to deserve all of what I was going through?

In my mind, I frequently pondered "why bad things would happen to good people?" I couldn't quite understand the logic behind it. I was unsure about everything that had happened to me. For instance, the sexual abuse that I went through, the abandonment of my biological father since birth, the loss of my two children, and the loss of my favorite cousin to cancer. I used to wonder all the time why I had to go through such traumatic situations. Pain from those situations stuck with me for a very long time. Knowing that none of them were my fault, still didn't make it any easier to get through.

I wouldn't wish any of the pain that I've experienced on anyone.

If you can relate to any of the situations that I have been through, I want u to know that God can heal you too, and He will without a doubt. You have to believe in God and in the power of His healing because it's real and does exist.

The reason I was going through so many challenges were beyond my understanding. None of us know the answers to everything, but God knows. I was tired of being confused, so I went to God in prayer and asked Him to bring clarity. I wanted Him to help me to understand why we as people go through challenges in our lives. I really needed to know because at that point I had already dealt with what I thought was enough, and I needed healing.

I had to go to God for healing on numerous occasions. I would cry out to Him and express how hurt I was and how I was feeling. God already knew how I felt, but He is my Father, so a part of having a relationship with Him, is expressing how I feel. God definitely has healed me in ways that I didn't think were possible. I occasionally look back on my life and see how much I have persevered.

God has healed me tremendously and helped me to see the good in it all.

First and foremost, a tremendous part of receiving God's healing, is understanding forgiveness. One thing I can say about myself is that I am a forgiving person. I used to feel extremely stupid for forgiving the people who had hurt me. It was actually pretty embarrassing to me how quickly I forgave. God stepped in and showed me that I shouldn't feel stupid for forgiving those who have hurt me. He whispered in my ear that I was doing the right thing.

He said that He was proud of me for my forgiving heart.

God forgives us for our sins, so we must also learn to forgive as well. I'm not saying it is always easy for me to forgive someone after being hurt because it's not, but I know I have to obey God and exercise forgiveness.

I have forgiven the people who abused me sexually, deceived me, lied to me, abandoned me, cursed me, stole from me, and the list goes on. Of course, forgiving all of these people was a hard thing to do, but with God's help I was able to do so. I pray that they were able to forgive themselves as well for what they did to me. Being such a forgiving person has carried me pretty far in life.

Grudges develop when you fail to forgive, as the bible instructs you to do.

I really had to exercise forgiveness when I went through the devastation of losing my daughter Layla Amerie and my son Jordan Royal. I had to forgive myself and also God. I had to forgive myself because losing them wasn't my fault in any way. I had to forgive God because everything happens for His good and He doesn't make any mistakes. I admit that I was upset with God for several reasons. First, I know that He knew how bad I wanted children of my own. Second, I knew how much of an amazing mother I would have been to Layla and Jordan. Third, I could not believe I had given birth to two beautiful babies who didn't survive. I have to admit that I was at the point where I was ready to check out on life. The pain was too much for me to deal with. I had no idea what to do and how to move on. Being angry with God didn't help. I had always loved children and wanted to have my very own. Then to lose both due to preterm labor made me question life itself. I had to let go and forgive. That's when I entered a path and journey of healing in my life. I cried out to God and told Him how much I loved Him and how sorry I was for being angry with Him. I'm here to tell you that an extremely heavy load was lifted off of me.

I felt so much better and was ready to experience His true healing.

I made an important decision in my life to seek God diligently and to strive to get closer to Him. In getting closer to Him, He gave me an abundance of peace, strength, comfort, and healing. He gave me all of those things and much more. I wanted to question Him about everything that was going on in my life, but I knew that I wasn't supposed to question His doings. However, I did ask for understanding.

He gave me a better insight on why we go through challenges in life. He reminded me that life wasn't meant to be easy! He also reminded me of one of His promises to never ever leave me nor forsaken me, and that He will forever be there for the rest of the days of my life! I took a moment to think back over my life and He has never left me nor forsaken me. God has always remained with me through everything that I have gone through.

Can you relate to this? Wouldn't you agree that no matter what you've been through in your life, that God has never left you nor forsaken you? Take a moment to think back over your life.

Follow me on this 30-day journey.

DAY 1
EVERYONE FACES
CHALLENGES IN LIFE

In life, we all go through challenges, and no one on the planet is excluded from that fact.

Primarily, we live in an imperfect world, therefore challenges are bound to arise daily.

Secondly, we as humans are also imperfect and will never be, no matter how hard we try.

Thirdly, the world is filled with all types of temptation and sin.

Fourthly, we must understand that some things are caused by the evil spirits that exist. We are not fighting against flesh and blood, but demons and principalities.

We will forever be faced with challenges in our lives. We may not go through the exact same trials in life as others do, but it's inevitable that we will at some point in life be faced with something difficult that we must overcome in order to grow. On the outside looking in, it may seem that your challenges are tougher than the trials that you see others go through. You may often find yourself asking, "why me?" Who determines who's tough enough to handle certain difficulties anyway?

Different people deal with challenges differently. One thing to remember is that God never said life would be easy.

Two people going through very similar situations are going to deal with them differently. God designed all of us and we are all unique in our own way.

Life throws us all types of curve balls. Some of us more than others have to face adversities on a daily basis. One minute things could be going extremely well, and the next minute, extremely terrible. The thing about it is, you never know when things are going to change. Often, things change quickly. You have to always be ready for any and everything. I'm sure you've heard the phrase, "if you stay ready, you don't have to get ready!" You have to go with the flow in life and expect the unexpected.

Unexpected things happen in life every single day, which keeps us on our toes. Things in life are not always going to go your way, and it's important to realize this.

I used to have a tough time realizing that some things just weren't going to go my way. As I came to understand this, I had a revelation. My entire way of thinking and mindset changed for the better. I started to understand better that some unexpected things would happen, and to just stay ready.

I have noticed that I have the ability to sense something about to take place, before it actually happens. I like to call it my sixth sense, which is discernment from God.

Having discernment from God became an enormous help. Being more in tuned with Him allows you to have discernment. I also accepted the fact that circumstances can change at the drop of a dime. Changes take place all the time, whether they are for good or bad.

The types of challenges in life that one can be faced with are countless. Some people often seem shocked that a certain thing has happened to them.

I am here to tell you that anything can happen to absolutely anyone. Unimaginable things might happen in your life; it's how you handle them that makes you stronger. No one is ever exempt from anything happening to them.

In life people go through all types of challenges from financial hardships, to having too much money and still being miserable, to wanting a better job or career, weight gain, weight loss, from not liking their physical appearance, to self-esteem issues, sexual abuse, from a disease, to personal illness, miscarriages or stillborn, needing help with raising a disabled child, single parenthood, marital issues, a spouse away in the military, divorce, loss of a loved one, acceptance, jealousy, envy, having a learning disability, coping with addictions, codependency, and the list goes on. Often times, these challenges are independent of each other. But some of us we may have to face several of them all at the exact same time.

But keep in mind, just because you go through these challenges, it doesn't mean that you are a bad person. You must continue to remind yourself of that.

Some of the challenges that we are faced with cannot be explained. God knows what you can bare and get through. He would never put too much on you than you can handle. If your plate is full then, He knows how strong of a person you are.

One of my favorite people in the Bible is a man by the name of Job. Job was an extremely strong man. His strength to me was very impressive. He was hit with some tough challenges that some of us wouldn't be able to bare. Job lost all of his possessions and children, yet he still remained faithful to God. In fact, he still praised God through the midst of it all. Satan tried to test Job's faith because he wanted to prove that Job's faith was conditional and only based upon God blessing him. However, Job continued to praise God and Satan was proved wrong. Eventually God rewarded and blessed Job with way more than he had before.

You and I should also keep praising God each and every time we face adversity as well. We have to surrender to God, praise Him, and to bring glory to His name. Don't just call on His Holy name when you need Him during times of struggle and troubled times, but also be willing to praise Him and thank Him when faced with adversity. Thank Him for all of the good times and all of the bad times you encounter. Having this approach about life will make the challenges you face much easier to get though.

LESSON
Everyone goes through challenges in life. Bring glory to God's name in the midst of good times and also during bad times.

2 Corinthians 4:8 NIV

"We are hard pressed on every side, but not crushed; perplexed, but not in despair."

Deuteronomy 4:30-31 NIV

"When you are in distress and all these things have happened to you, then in later days you will return to The Lord your God and obey him.

For the LORD your God is a merciful God; he will not abandon or destroy you or forget the covenant with your ancestors, which he confirmed to them by oath."

2 Samuel 22:7-8 NIV

"In my distress I called to the LORD; I called out to my God. From his temple he heard my voice; my cry came to his ears. The earth trembled and quaked, the foundations of the heavens shook; they trembled because he was angry."

SOMETHING TO THINK ABOUT

Today, think about some challenges that you have faced in your life. How did you get through them?

1. _____
   _____
   _____

2. _____
   _____
   _____

3. _____
   _____
   _____

PRAYER

Father, I thank you for allowing me to go through challenges in life. I thank you for not letting me go through them alone. Thank you for being with me and remaining by my side through it all. Please bring me comfort, guidance and peace. Amen.

MY THOUGHTS ON THIS LESSON

_____

_____

_____

_____

_____

_____

_____

_____

_____

_____

_____

_____

_____

_____

_____

_____

_____

_____

_____

_____

_____

_____

_____

_____

_____

_____

_____

_____

_____

DAY 2
GOD COMMUNICATES WITH YOU

God has His own way of showing us different things that He wants us to see. You and I might often feel as if He is showing us something in a harsh way. But, God has a reason behind everything and means well by the things we go through. We might not understand at that particular time what He is doing and why He is doing it, but He will bring clarity. He will help us understand what He is trying to get through to us and what He wants us to hear. You have to pay attention and listen to what He is saying to you because He will tell you - in time.

God has His ways of communicating to us and letting us know different things that we need to know, so we have to pay close attention. During our challenges, He is communicating with us even when we think He is not.

You may hear many different voices, which may confuse you, so pay attention so you won't be misled by other voices. There are many voices playing in our heads and I'm sure you are aware of that. Be a good judge in distinguishing which voice is God's voice, the only one to listen to. The enemy is definitely one of the voices that's competing to be heard. The enemy's plan is to try to get you to doubt

God and the relationship that you have with Him.

Dealing with life and being busy with work and family can be a major hindrance in hearing Him and can cause you to miss your message from God. Living in the times that we do, makes hearing from God more challenging than it used to be. With all of the entertainment, internet, and social media that we have access to now, it's easy to tune God out even when we are not trying to do so. Other things gain our focus and we miss out on hearing Him. You cannot fall victim to this, so develop a closer relationship with God and be more in tuned with Him and hearing His voice.

God communicates with us in numerous ways, and the goal is to not miss out on any sources of His ways of communication. One common way of hearing Him is through scripture.

I hear God speaking to me all the time. I hear Him instructing me to do different things. I don't always agree with everything He is telling me, but I definitely hear Him. He communicates with me in a way that makes me aware of particular things that I need to watch out for and for my protection. I hear Him daily reminding me of things such as something that I might be walking out of the house without. Or when He tells me to switch lanes and I later notice an accident in the opposite lane further up the road. People often compare this to following your first mind, which is God speaking to you. I always praise and give Him thanks for giving me direction to follow because it is a beautiful thing to experience.

God speaks to us through other people as well. Often times other people hear from God about us, and they share it with us.

I recently met a lady who told me that God told her something in regards to my future marriage. She swept me off my feet as she began telling me what God told her. The interesting thing is, God had already given me a similar revelation. I shockingly asked her several times how did she know this information and she told me that God told her. She was a very kind hearted lady and being in her presence, you could tell that she had an anointing. There are many people like her who have a special anointing. I've been told that I also do too, in which I also believe. Take notice of those people in your life.

God also uses dreams and visions to communicate with us. I often experience both of these communication outlets as well. A good amount of the dreams that I've had, have actually came true, or close to being true. For example, I've had several dreams about my close female friends becoming pregnant, and they actually became pregnant. Or having a dream being warned about people to stay away from who are no good for me. I have to admit that it is sometimes a little frightening to experience, but in actuality there is nothing to be afraid of. I have learned that it is another form of communication from my Father.

When I was twenty years old I kept having visions about the number twenty and I sensed death. I started to panic because I wasn't sure if it was going to be me or a loved one close to me. About a month or so later the unthinkable happened. A close friend of mine passed away. I kept having visions about the number twenty because she passed away on January twentieth at three twenty pm on highway I-20, and she would've turned twenty years old that year. It was a tough situation to deal with and took me a long time to get through because she was like a little sister to me. God rest her soul.

THE LESSON

God has many ways of communicating with us. Tune in and pay close attention to Him.

John 10:27 NIV

"My sheep listen to my voice; I know them, and they follow me."

John 8:47 NIV

"Whoever belongs to God hears what God says. The reason you do not hear is that you do not belong to God."

Isaiah 50:4 NIV

"The Sovereign LORD has given me a well-instructed tongue, to know the word that sustains the weary.
He wakens me morning by morning, wakens my ear to listen like one being instructed."

SOMETHING TO THINK ABOUT

Today, think about a time God communicated with you. How did He communicate with you and what did He tell you?

1. _____
   _____
   _____

2. _____
   _____
   _____

3. _____
   _____
   _____

PRAYER

Father, help me to understand that you want to communicate with me and that you have many different ways of doing so. Let me know how much you want me to hear from you. You have a say so in everything and you want me to be aware of it. I know that in order to follow you, I need to be able to hear you clearly. Show me ways I can communicate with you better. Bring me clarity, understanding, and knowledge of what you are teaching me. Thank you. Amen.

MY THOUGHTS ON THIS LESSON

_____

_____

_____

_____

_____

_____

_____

_____

_____

_____

_____

_____

_____

_____

_____

_____

_____

_____

_____

_____

_____

_____

_____

_____

_____

_____

_____

_____

JOURNEY SPEAKS

_____

_____

_____

_____

_____

_____

_____

_____

_____

_____

_____

_____

_____

_____

_____

_____

_____

_____

DAY 3
FULL ARMOR OF GOD

God designed challenges to be a part of an experience in your life. When you go through challenges, He is teaching you something. A part of His training includes molding, shaping and forming you into who He designed you to be. God is your teacher. In a way, He is your sergeant and is training you for what is similar to war. This is a tough world we live in and you need to be strong to survive. Put on your full armor of God. Not only put it on but actually use it because you're going to need it.

The phrase "full armor of God" comes from Ephesians 6:13-17: "Therefore put on the full armor of God, so that when the day of evil comes, you may be able to stand your ground, and after you have done everything, to stand. Stand firm then, with the belt of truth buckled around your waist, with the breastplate of righteousness in place, and with your feet fitted with the readiness that comes from the gospel of peace. In addition to all this, take up the shield of faith, with which you can extinguish all the flaming arrows of the evil one. Take the helmet of salvation and the sword of the Spirit, which is the word of God."

Ephesians 6:12, clearly indicates that the conflict with Satan is spiritual, and therefore no tangible weapons can be effectively employed against him and his minions. We are not given a list of specific tactics Satan will use. However, the passage is quite clear that when we follow all the instructions faithfully, we will be able to stand, and we will have victory regardless of Satan's strategy.

In Ephesians 6: verse 14, we are told to "put on the breastplate of righteousness." A breastplate shielded a warrior's vital organs from blows that would otherwise be fatal. This righteousness is not works of righteousness done by men. Rather, this is the righteousness of Christ, imputed by God and received by faith, which guards our hearts against the accusations and charges of Satan and secures our innermost being from his attacks.

Allow God to prepare you as much as He needs to before going to war. He is preparing you for survival. He wants you to be strong so that you can withstand any and everything that comes your way. Only the strong will survive.

THE LESSON
Through your challenges, God is training and preparing you for things in life.

Hebrews 13:21 NIV

"equip you with everything good for doing his will, and may he work in us what is pleasing to him, through Jesus Christ, to whom be glory for ever and ever. Amen."

Ephesians 2:10 NIV

"For we are God's handiwork, created in Christ Jesus to do good works, which God prepared in advance for us to do."

Psalm 32:8-9 NIV

"I will instruct you and teach you in the way you should go; I will counsel you with my loving eye on you. Do not be like the horse or the mule, which have no understanding but must be controlled by bit and bridle or they will not come to you."

SOMETHING TO THINK ABOUT

Today, reflect on how God has trained and prepared you through challenges. What has He taught you?

1. _____
   _____
   _____

2. _____
   _____
   _____

3. _____
   _____
   _____

PRAYER

Father, I thank you for taking the time to teach me what I need to know. Thank you for building me up and making me stronger. Continue to prepare me in whatever way you need to. I trust in you and what you have designed for my life. Amen.

MY THOUGHTS ON THIS LESSON

_____
_____
_____
_____
_____
_____
_____
_____
_____
_____
_____
_____
_____
_____
_____
_____
_____

JOURNEY SPEAKS

DAY 4
PERSEVERANCE

God wants you to be able to persevere, which leads to eternal salvation. The ability to persevere isn't easy, but it can be done. In order to persevere you have to make a decision that you will keep pushing to get through any and all of the challenges you may be faced with. Despite all of the obstacles that may get in the way, you must stay determined to keep pushing.

Perseverance is key to continuance grace to the end. You have the power to overcome all challenges that come your way. Repeatedly tell yourself that you have the power to make it through. God will see you through any and everything you face in life.

I had to trust that God would see me through the loss of my job a couple of months ago. Losing my job felt like a bad dream that I wanted to wake up from. It didn't seem real for me, especially since I had just gotten a raise and was making pretty good money. It happened out of nowhere. I had a vision months before it happened that I wouldn't be there for a long time. Since I had just gotten a raise, I figured that I would work for a few more months, save more money, look for another full time job, and then put in my two weeks' notice.

Panic tends to be the first reaction when something drastic happens. I went from working forty plus hours a week at that job, to working zero hours in a blink of an eye. It was a very scary situation because I depended on that job as my main source of income. On top of losing that job, the company did not pay me my last two paychecks. So not only did I no longer have a full time job, I didn't receive any of the money that was owed to me for my work. After a few days of panic, I looked to the word of God. Believing that God would see me through as He did with everything else, I knew that without a doubt that He would make a way. I was unsure of what exactly would happen and what strings He would pull to make this come together. But I reminded myself that I am His daughter and that He loves me unconditionally. I also reminded myself that He is Jehovah Jireh my only provider.

He knows what we need before we even ask. Our needs are already met by Him before hand and that's something we need to constantly remind ourselves of and never forget.

I knew that especially in a time of need that He wouldn't leave me with no sense of direction. I read His word and it reminded me of the promises He gave to me. I suggest you also hold onto His promises and don't let the enemy make you think anything different.

Even when your hope is gone continue to hold onto His promises. Believe that He will turn things around for you even when it doesn't seem like He will. Have faith in Him and believe in Him.

I made a decision to only rely on God one hundred percent during this tough time. I didn't want to rely on anyone for anything besides Him. Go to God first and foremost with your needs. He will always provide for you and will never disappoint you nor mislead you. Put all of your trust in Him.

The result of my situation turned out extremely well and once again, I made it through. God brought me through and He showed up and showed out for me big time. I didn't go without anything and He took excellent care of me. He made a way when there seemed to be absolutely no way.

THE LESSON

With God's help, you have the power to overcome challenges that come your way.

Philippians 4:13 NIV

"I can do all this through him who gives me strength."

Jeremiah 29:11 NIV

*"For I know the plans I have for you," declares the L*ORD*, "plans to prosper you and not to harm you, plans to give you hope and a future."*

Psalm 23:1-2 NIV

*"The L*ORD *is my shepherd, I lack nothing. He makes me lie down in green pastures, he leads me beside quiet waters."*

SOMETHING TO THINK ABOUT

Today, think about a time you had to persevere.

What are some things that helped you persevere?

1. _____

   _____

   _____

2. _____

   _____

   _____

3. _____

   _____

   _____

PRAYER

Father, I thank you for persistence. Thank you for showing me that I too can persevere. Thank you for allowing me to get through challenges in life. Thank you for your guidance. Continue to direct my path. Amen.

MY THOUGHTS ON THIS LESSON

_____

_____

_____

_____

_____

_____

_____

_____

_____

_____

_____

_____

_____

_____

_____

_____

DAY 5
CHALLENGES & YOUR
EMOTIONS

Depending on what type of challenge you are facing, several different emotions are sure to arise. You may feel mad, sad, angry, confused, jealous, envious, or alone. There is no right or wrong way to feel and no one can tell you how you should feel. At times you may go through a series of emotions, which is completely normal. You may even feel all of the emotions at once, and it may be difficult to know how to react.

Most people feel alone when they are going through challenges. I know all too well how it feels. Feeling alone takes a lot out of you and can be hard to shake at times. You often feel like you are the only one going through a particular challenge and that no one else understands. Especially, if loved ones and friends have never been through the same situation before. They can only pin point how you might be feeling, but will never really know exactly. Trying to put themselves in your shoes to relate, still does not give a clear understanding.

When I lost my children, due to preterm labor, I went through several different types of emotions. Some of the emotions I couldn't even begin to explain. In the beginning, I felt very angry, which led to a state of confusion, pain, sadness, feeling alone and the list of emotions goes on. I felt alone because I thought no one understood what I was going through and how traumatic losing my children was. I guess I couldn't expect many people to understand what I was going through if they've never loss a child before. Or in my case, experience the loss of two children in the same year. Getting through the loss of my children was rough on me but, I had God. In actuality I was never alone because God never left my side.

We are never alone and shouldn't feel such a way. God is always with us blessing us with His presence. Lean on Him and let Him comfort you because His love is always available to you. All you have to do is go to Him and seek Him first.

I started to lean on God more and started seeking Him diligently. I started diving into His word more and making a strong effort to find out more of who He is. I even fasted and prayed to get better results and to feel closer to Him.

If you haven't already, make an effort to spend more time with God. Give Him the first of your time each day. When He blesses you to open your eyes and live another day, thank Him and give Him praise. He wants to spend time with you and He deserves quality time. Invite Him into your life and start to seek Him diligently.

THE LESSON
God is always with you during your challenges.

Joshua 1:5 NIV

"No one will be able to stand against you all the days of your life. As I was with Moses, so I will be with you; I will never leave you nor forsake you."

John 14:18 NIV

"I will not leave you as orphans; I will come to you."

Isaiah 41:10 NIV

"So do not fear, for I am with you; do not be dismayed, for I am your God. I will strengthen you and help you; I will uphold you with my righteous right hand."

Isaiah 41:13 NIV

*"For I am the L*ORD *your God who takes hold of your right hand and says to you, do not fear; I will help you."*

SOMETHING TO THINK ABOUT

Today, reflect on a time you felt alone.

Describe how God showed you that you weren't alone, and that He was right there with you.

1. _____
   _____
   _____

2. _____
   _____
   _____

3. _____
   _____
   _____

PRAYER

Father, I thank you for being with me. Thank you for not leaving me to be alone. Forgive me for putting pressure on loved ones who don't understand what I am going through. Allow me to seek you first instead of others. Amen.

MY THOUGHTS ON THIS LESSON

_____
_____
_____
_____
_____
_____
_____
_____
_____
_____
_____
_____
_____
_____
_____
_____
_____
_____

JOURNEY SPEAKS

Day 6
LEARN SOMETHING FROM YOUR CHALLENGES

Challenges in life teach you many different things. Through losing my children, God taught me an array of things. He taught me to trust in Him first and foremost. Secondly, He provided me with the strength that I need. He taught me to remain strong. I have always been a strong woman, but I gained more strength through my loss. I never would have been able to imagine my level of strength in going through something as drastic as the loss of my children, but God brought me through.

At times I still look back and know that it was only because of God that I got through things. Even though God built me strong, it wasn't my own strength that brought me through. God's strength brought me though without a doubt. He helped me to also experience a level of healing that I needed. I went from laying in the bed crying everyday all day, to gaining strength. If it wasn't for God I never would've made it. Gradually I started to get out of my bed wanting to do better and wanting His healing. I knew that my life wasn't complete and that He still had a divine purpose for my life. Laying in the bed crying every day would not make living out my purpose possible. I mean there is nothing wrong with grieving, it's normal. However, something in me wanted to persevere and make it to the next level in life. Of course all that took time and didn't happen overnight.

Discipline is also taught from going through challenges in life. Discipline is an important factor in life. We all need a little discipline from time to time. Without discipline we wouldn't take life serious and wouldn't be able to grow and learn from our mistakes. Just like parents have to teach their children through discipline. The Bible teaches about discipline as well. God teaches us through discipline because we are His children. Discipline although sometimes painful, is for our own good. It produces a harvest of righteousness and peace for those who have been trained by it. In order to get to the next level in life we must embrace discipline through our challenges that our Heavenly Father allows us to face.

LESSON
God is your Father, therefore He teaches you through discipline.

Hebrews 12:4-12 NIV

"In your struggle against sin, you have not yet resisted to the point of shedding your blood. And have you completely forgotten this word of encouragement that addresses you as a father addresses his son? It says,

My son, do not make light of the Lord's discipline, and do not lose heart when he rebukes you, because the Lord disciplines the one he loves, and he chastens everyone he accepts as his son.

Endure hardship as discipline; God is treating you as his children. For what children are not disciplined by their father? If you are not disciplined—and everyone undergoes discipline—then you are not legitimate, not true sons and daughters at all. Moreover, we have all had human fathers who disciplined us and we respected them for it. How much more should we submit to the Father of spirits and live! They disciplined us for a little while as they thought best; but God disciplines us for our good, in order that we may share in his holiness. No discipline seems pleasant at the time, but painful. Later on, however, it produces a harvest of righteousness and peace for those who have been trained by it. Therefore, strengthen your feeble arms and weak knees."

SOMETHING TO THINK ABOUT

Today, think about a time God disciplined you. What are some things that you learned through His discipline?

1. _____
   _____
   _____

2. _____
   _____
   _____

3. _____
   _____
   _____

PRAYER

Father, thank you for allowing me to be more dependent on you. I cannot do anything with my strength alone, therefore I have to lean on you. Thank you for your discipline. Your discipline although sometimes painful, is for my good. Discipline me in other areas that I am in need. Amen.

MY THOUGHTS ON THIS LESSON

_____

_____

_____

_____

_____

_____

_____

_____

_____

_____

_____

_____

_____

_____

_____
_____
_____
_____
_____
_____
_____
_____
_____
_____
_____
_____
_____
_____
_____
_____
_____
_____
_____
_____
_____
_____
_____
_____
_____
_____

DAY 7
CHARACTER DEVELOPMENT

When you go through challenges in life, most often it may change you. Your character is shaped by the things that you go through and things you're faced with. Character development is a tremendous part of growth. Growth and changes are a part of life and we gain a better understanding of life itself through them. Knowledge and wisdom are rewards of growth and development in the shaping of your character.

Through my favorite cousin's passing, I learned a lot. It was an extremely tough situation to deal with. I was made more aware of death, and I began to understand more that we all are going to pass on one day. I learned to not take living another day for granted. The truth is that we as people don't live forever. People have passed on last night and didn't get a chance to wake up this morning. Unfortunately, we don't know when our time will expire. Living forever on Earth just isn't possible.

Another character developer is that our faith in God strengthens from challenges. We begin to trust in Him more and more. We begin to lean on His understanding and not our own.

I trusted that God's will had been done in my cousin's life. I also trusted that God had allowed my cousin to live out his purpose before he passed. We have to put our trust in God at all times. God is a faithful God and He is faithful at all times. He is even faithful when we don't think He is.

LESSON
Your character is shaped through challenges that you face.

Romans 5:4-13 NIV

"perseverance, character; and character, hope. And hope does not put us to shame, because God's love has been poured out into our hearts through the Holy Spirit, who has been given to us.

You see, at just the right time, when we were still powerless, Christ died for the ungodly. Very rarely will anyone die for a righteous person, though for a good person someone might possibly dare to die. But God demonstrates his own love for us in this: While we were still sinners, Christ died for us. Since we have now been justified by his blood, how much more shall we be saved from God's wrath through him! For if, while we were God's enemies, we were reconciled to him through the death of his Son, how much more, having been reconciled, shall we be saved through his life! Not only is this so, but we also boast in God through our Lord Jesus Christ, through whom we have now received reconciliation."

SOMETHING TO THINK ABOUT

Today, think about a time God shaped your character through a challenge.

How was it shaped?

1. _____
   _____
   _____

2. _____
   _____
   _____

3. _____
   _____
   _____

PRAYER

Father, thank you for shaping my character. I've realized how important it is. I appreciate the strength that I have gained. Please continue to strengthen me. Amen.

MY THOUGHTS ON THIS LESSON

_____

_____

_____

_____

_____

_____

_____

_____

_____

_____

_____

_____

_____

_____

_____

_____

DAY 8
STOP COMPARING YOUR
CHALLENGES TO OTHERS

Making comparisons about your life to other people's lives is something that you should not do. It's not advantageous to make comparisons about the challenges you face because we all go through them, one way or another. With anything in life, do not get in the habit of comparing yourselves to others. Some people feel often like God is allowing more sufferings in their life more so than others. Everything happens in accordance to God's will, so it's not your place to judge.

I used to wonder why women who didn't want kids, had them. I also used to wonder why women were blessed with kids, but then treat them bad. I've also thought about the mothers and father who have left their kids in a hot car to die. I've also spent time thinking about those who have been abusive and beat their kids to death. Situations like these never sat right with me because I lost my children. Everyone who knows me says I would've been an amazing mother to my children. I would have never done any harm to them in any shape or form had their lives been spared.

Of course, it's a natural reaction to wonder why those type of women had kids, but I had to lose mine. However, it wasn't healthy for me to compare their lives to my own. The answer was beyond my understanding. No one knows the answer to a question like that. Only God knows. It is not our place to question God but we are human. We have to learn to trust in Him even when we don't understand. He doesn't make any mistakes at all.

God has a plan for everyone's life and He knows what will take place in each one of our lives from beginning to the very end. He knows what we can and can't bare, and will never put more on us than we can bare. He knows what each one of us can withstand. If it appears that you are going through more than others than He might just have a greater calling for your life. The more challenges you experience means that you will have an even bigger testimony in the end.

LESSON
God has a unique plan for your life, therefore your challenges will differ from others.

Galatians 6:4-6 NIV

"Each one should test their own actions. Then they can take pride in themselves alone, without comparing themselves to someone else, for each one should carry their own load. [6] Nevertheless, the one who receives instruction in the word should share all good things with their instructor."

2 Corinthians 10:12 NIV

"We do not dare to classify or compare ourselves with some who commend themselves. When they measure themselves by themselves and compare themselves with themselves, they are not wise."

SOMETHING TO THINK ABOUT

Today, think about how important it is to not compare your challenges.

What are some reasons why you shouldn't?

1. _____
   _____
   _____

2. _____
   _____
   _____

3. _____
   _____
   _____

PRAYER

Father, help me not compare my life to others. Help me to understand that the challenges that I face are meant to help me grow. Help me to be grateful for the life that you have given me. Help me to focus on my own life, instead of making comparisons to others. Amen.

MY THOUGHTS ON THIS LESSON

_____

_____

_____

_____

_____

_____

_____

_____

_____

_____

_____

_____

_____

_____

DAY 9
REMAIN IN YOUR LANE

A part of remaining in your lane is to start focusing better. Staying focused however, can be difficult. Focusing and not losing sight will help you to stay on track and accomplish amazing things.

I had to remain in my lane and focus better after losing my children. I had to make more of an effort to focus on things concerning me rather than things that didn't concern me. I had to find a way to regroup and receive God's healing. I also had to properly grieve and come to realization that they were no longer here with me anymore.

It was challenging to remain focused on what was going on with me because I am a very caring person. I tend to focus a lot on others and their wellbeing. These are good qualities to have, but at that time I had to focus on me and seek God for emotional healing. I had to prioritize things in my life, and figure out what was best for me. I had to get to know myself all over again. When traumatic situations occur in your life, you may recognize a shift in your attitude.

I noted that there was a slight change in my attitude. I was often irritable and didn't really feel like doing much. I knew I had to focus on changing that because that was unlike me. I am an extremely outgoing person, so not wanting to get out of bed was unlike me. After some time, I begin to feel like myself again. Staying focused, and seeking God helped me to stay on track.

The quickest way to get off track is to lose focus, by concerning yourself with other people and things. Try hard not let the enemy get you side tracked. Remind yourself daily to stay on track and get in the practice of it. After a while, staying focused will become second nature to you.

Remaining in your lane is most definitely easier said than done and we all know that. It is easy to get sidetracked when you start worrying about what's going on in other people's lives. Gossiping can also knock you off track. Trying to keep up with the Jones's can also be a major distraction.

Take steps in making strides in this area of your life. Make it happen! Get a hold of the situation before things get out of hand.

LESSON
Stay focused and do not lose sight.

Philippians 3:13-14 NIV

"Brothers and sisters, I do not consider myself yet to have taken hold of it. But one thing I do: Forgetting what is behind and straining toward what is ahead, I press on toward the goal to win the prize for which God has called me heavenward in Christ Jesus."

Colossians 3:2

"Set your minds on things above, not on earthly things."

SOMETHING TO THINK ABOUT

Today, think about how important it is to stay focused and to not lose sight.

What are some things that you can do to focus better?

1. _____
   _____
   _____

2. _____
   _____
   _____

3. _____
   _____
   _____

PRAYER

Father, help me to focus better. Help me to stay focused on remaining in my lane. Show me the importance of prioritizing things in my life. Allow me to incorporate them in my daily life. Amen.

MY THOUGHTS ON THIS LESSON

_____

_____

_____

_____

_____

_____

_____

_____

_____

_____

_____

_____

_____

_____

_____

_____

_____
_____
_____
_____
_____
_____
_____
_____
_____
_____
_____
_____
_____
_____
_____
_____
_____
_____
_____
_____
_____
_____
_____
_____

DAY 10
GOD IS IN CONTROL

At times challenges can be exactly what you may need. More often, we rely on ourselves and think we can handle it all. We tend to think we are in control of our lives, when the exact opposite is true.

Losing my job showed me that God was in control, and that He always will be. He also showed me that He was in control of my well-being. I thought that my wellbeing was contingent upon my job. I learned first-hand once again that He is Jehovah Jireh, my provider, not the job I was working at. As His daughter, He has promised to provide and take care of me. He never left my side and I never went a day without food nor shelter or anything that I needed. God has provided everything that I needed and more.

I have a five-year-old dog named Day~Z and she's more like my baby and everyone knows how much I love and care about her. I love how sweet and lovable she is and it's hard for anyone not to fall in love with her after being around her too. She is very spoiled and I wonder how that happened?! I'm just kidding, I know exactly how she got spoiled and it's because of me. She has me wrapped around her little paw and she gets whatever she wants. She has a full wardrobe of clothes because I like to dress her up. She goes to the pet hotel to stay overnight when I travel out of town and the people that work there absolutely love her. I'm the kind of pet parent that calls at least twice a day to check on her and to get a report on how she's doing. They're used to it, and have a full report waiting for me. I got her the same year that I lost my children and Day~Z has been my therapy dog ever since.

Before I lost my job I had scheduled a surgery for Day~Z. She needed two procedures done in the same day. The first procedure was getting her fixed and the second procedure was getting a mass removal. Pretty much she had a lump on her breast and we needed to figure out what it was. I was nervous about both procedures and grew afraid of what would happen and what the outcome would be.

After losing my job, I had no idea how I was going to pay for Day~Z's surgery. Both procedures together we're almost four hundred dollars. At the time I couldn't spare the money because I had all of my bills coming up for the next month. I had no idea what I was going to do, so I cried out to God in hopes of a miracle. I knew that God would work things out for us, but I wasn't sure how he would do it. Well, God being the awesome God that He is, surely worked everything out. Two dog foundations blessed me with grants for Day~Z's procedures. The procedures were paid-in-full, less than the twenty-five- dollar deposit that I paid. She successfully went through both procedures and did well without any complications. By me not working full time, I was able to be home with her during her recovery process and tend to her every need. Her doctor called me about a week later with results from the biopsy which was the news that I had been waiting on. She started off by saying that I had saved Day~Z's life by noticing something wasn't right with her swollen breast. She then went on to say that the mass that they removed was cancerous and that it was removed at the right time before things got bad. My eyes filled with tears that could fill an ocean and all I could do was praise God for seeing Day~ Z and me through this.

I was able to witness first hand once again that God is in control of everything. He is in control of every area of our lives. Challenges occur in our lives to remind us of who He is.

LESSON
God will show you that He is in control.

Proverbs 16:3-4 NIV

*"Commit to the L*ORD *whatever you do, and he will establish your plans. The L*ORD *works out everything to its proper end—even the wicked for a day of disaster."*

Isaiah 48:17 NIV

*"This is what the L*ORD *says— your Redeemer, the Holy One of Israel: I am the L*ORD *your God, who teaches you what is best for you, who directs you in the way you should go."*

SOMETHING TO THINK ABOUT

Today, reflect on a time that God showed you that He was in control.

How did He show you?

1. _____
   _____
   _____

2. _____
   _____
   _____

3. _____
   _____
   _____

PRAYER

Father, please forgive me for thinking that I am in control. Forgive me for not acknowledging enough that you control any and everything. Thank you for your gentle reminders. Allow me to get in the habit of believing that you are in control of all things. Amen.

MY THOUGHTS ON THIS LESSON

_____
_____
_____
_____
_____
_____
_____
_____
_____
_____
_____
_____
_____
_____
_____

JOURNEY SPEAKS

DAY 11

LET'S TALK ABOUT HUMILITY

Going through challenges makes you develop a sense of humility. Operating in that sense of humility is a necessity to get through your challenges.

Often times I have to remind myself of humility. Possessing the quality of humbleness will carry you far in life. Constantly pray and ask God to help you exercise humility. Humility is what took the devil and thirty Angels out of heaven.

In the Bible, humility or humbleness is a quality of being courteous and respectful of others. It is the opposite of aggressiveness, arrogance, boastfulness, and vanity. Rather than, "Me first," humility allows us to say, "No, you first, my friend." Humility is a quality that allows us go more than halfway to meet the needs and demands of others.

Humility is needed to live in peace and harmony. Being boastful and proud will lead you to a road of pure destruction.

Do you possess too much pride? Do you feel that you can do things all on your own? If this is so, why would you need God? God resists the proud, but gives grace to the humble.

LESSON
Humility can be developed from challenges in life.

Romans 12:3 NIV

"For by the grace given me I say to every one of you: Do not think of yourself more highly than you ought, but rather think of yourself with sober judgment, in accordance with the faith God has distributed to each of you."

Philippians 2:3 NIV

"Do nothing out of selfish ambition or vain conceit. Rather, in humility value others above yourselves"

SOMETHING TO THINK ABOUT

Today, think about a time that you could've practiced using humility.

What are some ways that you could've used it?

1. _____
   _____
   _____

2. _____
   _____
   _____

3. _____
   _____
   _____

PRAYER

Father, I thank you for creating humility and allowing me to experience it. Continue to give me a better understanding of it. Help me to become more humble and allow me to walk in humility for the rest of my days. Amen.

MY THOUGHTS ON THIS LESSON

_____
_____
_____
_____
_____
_____
_____
_____
_____
_____
_____
_____
_____
_____
_____
_____
_____
_____

_____
_____
_____
_____
_____
_____
_____
_____
_____
_____
_____
_____
_____
_____
_____
_____
_____
_____
_____
_____
_____

DAY 12
HAVE PATIENCE

When going through challenges we are forced to deal with many different things simultaneously. One of those things, is patience. Some of us are patient, and some of us could use a bit of help in that department. Patience is forced upon us through the challenges that we are faced with. However, we can develop a sense of even greater patience depending on how difficult each situation is.

I had to develop a sense of patience when it came to having children. I absolutely love children and always have. Growing up, my friends all thought that I would own a daycare because they witnessed the love I had for children. I've always had a nurturing and loving spirit and always wanted children of my own to experience the wonderful world of motherhood.

Losing my two children has caused me to be patient in that aspect. Through God's healing, I have learned to have more patience and to trust in Him more. I trust that my Heavenly Father will bless me with more children one day. I will not only raise them but I will pour the word of God into them at an early age. I plan to tell them how good He is, and how much He has brought me through. He knows the desires of my heart and I now can see that clearly. God has an amazing future for me and I choose to be patient and let His timing prevail.

Psalm 37:4 NIV

"Take delight in The Lord, and He will give you the desires of your heart."

At times we have absolutely no choice in being anything but patient. You don't know how long it will take until you will get on the other side of life's challenges, only God knows. Embrace patience and wait on Him. Pray and have faith that He will change what you are going through in His timing and on His watch. In the end you will come out much stronger than when you started because of your endurance.

LESSON
Challenges teach you patience.

James 5:7-11 NIV

"Be patient, then, brothers and sisters, until the Lord's coming. See how the farmer waits for the land to yield its valuable crop, patiently waiting for the autumn and spring rains. You too, be patient and stand firm, because the Lord's coming is near. Don't grumble against one another, brothers and sisters, or you will be judged. The Judge is standing at the door! Brothers and sisters, as an example of patience in the face of suffering, take the prophets who spoke in the name of the Lord. As you know, we count as blessed those who have persevered. You have heard of Job's perseverance and have seen what the Lord finally brought about. The Lord is full of compassion and mercy."

SOMETHING TO THINK ABOUT

Today, reflect on how you can exercise patience throughout the day.

What are some ways to help you?

1. _____
   _____
   _____

2. _____
   _____
   _____

3. _____
   _____
   _____

PRAYER

Father, thank you for teaching me to have patience. I realize that it is not always easy, but it is your way of teaching me many things. Thank you for the endurance to hold on. Please give me continued strength that I need to overcome. Amen.

MY THOUGHTS ON THIS LESSON

Day 13
THINGS REALLY DO HAPPEN
FOR A REASON

Come to the realization that things in life happen for a reason. I used to think that this statement was untrue, but I have learned that in fact it is true. As much as it hurts me to hear, I have to understand that my children didn't make it for a reason. I trust in God that it was for a good reason and I know that He doesn't make any mistakes at all.

However, I still can't believe that they had to leave me so early and that I didn't even get a chance to bond with them outside of the womb. I was only able to bond with them through rubbing my stomach, singing to them, talking to them, and praying for them. After birth I had the opportunity to hold them and take pictures that I will cherish forever.

Of course, I had their whole lives planned out, but I never got a chance to experience any of it. I had to experience leaving the hospital empty handed without either of them. I was pushed out of the hospital in a wheelchair with empty arms and baby-less twice in the same year. This was the most traumatic thing I had ever been through in my entire life. Imagine wanting something so bad, and having it taken away from you without notice.

The things that happened to me were supposed to happen, believe it or not. God allows things to happen in our lives that are often very difficult to understand. It takes a ton of faith, forgiveness, strength and prayer to get through; some more so than others.

With every challenge you have to come to a realization and accept that things do indeed happen for a reason. God knows what's best for you. He knows what you need and when you need it. Just because He doesn't give you what you want when you want it, doesn't mean that He won't bless you with it later on in life. God's perfect timing is better than your own because He won't give you something that you're not ready for. He wants to prepare you for your blessings, whether it is children, a new car, new house, a promotion, an increase in your finances, a new job, a new business, a husband or wife.

In conclusion make a decision that you want to overcome what you have been through because it was supposed to happen. Decide that you want healing and that you want to excel to a higher level. Make the changes required to move forward. Remaining stagnant in your situation is unhealthy and might cause depression if you don't take the proper steps to move forward.

Of course in some instances you will have to go through a grieving process, which takes some time.

Grieving is understandable, but making a decision to move forward is the result of growth.

When you go through life's challenges, you have the choice to either fall apart and become a victim of your circumstances, or you can rise up high and move forward.

LESSON
Everything in life happens for a reason.

Ecclesiastes 3:3-8 NIV

"To everything there is a season, and a time to every purpose under the heaven: A time to be born, and a time to die; a time to plant, and a time to pluck up that which is planted; A time to kill, and a time to heal; a time to break down, and a time to build up; A time to weep, and a time to laugh; a time to mourn, and a time to dance; A time to cast away stones, and a time to gather stones together; a time to

embrace, and a time to refrain from embracing; A time to get, and a time to lose; a time to keep, and a time to cast away; A time to rend, and a time to sew; a time to keep silence, and a time to speak; A time to love, and a time to hate; a time of war, and a time of peace."

Romans 8:28 NIV

"And we know that in all things God works for the good of those who love him, who have been called according to his purpose."

SOMETHING TO THINK ABOUT

Today, reflect on how everything in life happens for a reason.

How will you handle challenges differently?

1. _____
   _____
   _____

2. _____
   _____
   _____

3. _____
   _____
   _____

PRAYER

Father, thank you for allowing things to happen in my life. Although I may not understand at that moment, help me to realize it was for a reason. Thank you for designing everything in life to have a meaning. Help me to keep this in mind during the tough times. Keep me strong and let your strength reign upon me. Amen.

MY THOUGHTS ON THIS LESSON

_____

_____

_____

_____

_____

_____

_____

_____

_____

_____

_____

_____

_____

_____

_____

_____

_____

_____

JOURNEY SPEAKS

DAY 14
MOVING FORWARD IS
HEALTHY

As hard as it is, moving forward in life is a healthy thing to do. Moving forward allows healing and recovery to take place.

Some things we might not be able to completely get over in life, such as the loss of a loved one, but we can learn to get through things a little bit easier. With God anything is possible.

It took me a while to get through my favorite cousin's death. I didn't want to accept that he was gone. It took time to even process that he had been diagnosed with cancer in the first place. Imagine how hard it was to process that he was no longer here with me on Earth. He was more like a brother to me, rather than a first cousin. We talked on the phone every single day, at least two times at that. We would confide in each other and give advice to one another about things that we were going through. I truly trusted him. He was a great male figure for me and was one of the only few people that had never done anything to hurt me. He truly wanted the very best for me and he showed it often. He adored me like no other and losing him caused so much pain in my life. It broke my heart to get the call that he had passed away. I never thought that my heart would heal after losing him, but God definitely stepped in and brought healing.

God can heal our hearts and take the pain away with time. Trust and believe in Him that He can do so in your life. He can also help you see death in another light; as a time to rejoice. In the Bible it says that we are supposed to rejoice when a loved one passes away. It is easier said than done of course and is often very difficult to comprehend.

The sooner you heal and get through, the sooner you will be able to see the light again and move on with your life. Seeing the light again means that you will be able to live within the purpose that God has for your life.

Living in your purpose means that you are fulfilling your God given purpose in life. You should be living out your purpose and searching for what your calling is. If you are unsure what your purpose is, pray and ask God to reveal it to you. If you are having a tough time hearing from God, you may need to open up your heart to Him fully.

Go to God and ask Him what the reason for your existence is. Ask Him are you fulfilling the purpose that He has for your life. Also ask Him if the template of your life matches up with the template of glorious living because His design for you is to live gloriously. God has called you out of darkness into His marvelous light to fulfill a calling on your life.

LESSON

Moving forward allows you to experience healing. With God's help, you will be able to live within your purpose and calling.

Psalm 147:3 NIV

"He heals the brokenhearted and binds up their wounds."

Jeremiah 17:14 NIV

"Heal me, LORD, and I will be healed; save me and I will be saved, for you are the one I praise."

Jeremiah 29:11-13 NIV

"For I know the plans I have for you, declares the LORD, plans to prosper you and not to harm you, plans to give you hope and a future."

SOMETHING TO THINK ABOUT

Today, reflect on why moving forward is healthy.

What are some ways you can incorporate moving forward in your life?

1. _____
   _____
   _____

2. _____
   _____
   _____

3. _____
   _____
   _____

PRAYER

Father, thank you for giving me the strength to move forward. Thank you for your healing. Thank you for giving me the ability to experience true healing that can only come from you. Reveal to me my purpose and calling in life. Make them crystal clear. Amen

MY THOUGHTS ON THIS LESSON

_____

_____

_____

_____

_____

_____

_____

_____

_____

_____

_____

_____

_____

_____

_____

_____

_____

JOURNEY SPEAKS

DAY15
EVEN CHRISTIANS GO THROUGH CHALLENGES IN LIFE

No one on Earth is exempt from going through trials and tribulations in life. Many people think that being a Christian will make you exempt from the challenges that non-believers face, but this is not the case. You can search the Bible and see that it doesn't mention anywhere that believers will be exempt from hardships. All of us will go through challenges, those that are both good and bad.

When I was young in Christ I made an assumption that I would go through less misfortunes in my life since I was saved. In my mind I truly felt that hurdles would lessen because I became a Christian. I was in for a rude awakening and caught on pretty quickly.

Satan will put people in your life to confuse and mislead you. He is out to steal, kill and destroy your life, and form weapons against. Speak God's word over your life and believe that no weapon formed against you will prosper.

Have you ever wondered why God doesn't make your life easy? Or why He takes things away from you as He did Job in the Bible? The Bible reminds us that we are His children and He indeed loves us very much.

God has a timeline of events that will happen in your life. Everything has a divine purpose. The challenges that you face are for your good and He wants the best for you. His plan is to bless you tremendously. Make yourself available for His blessings.

LESSON
Even Christians go through challenges in life.

Philippians 4:19 NIV

"And my God will supply every need of yours according to His riches in glory in Christ Jesus."

1 Peter 1:6-8 NIV

"In all this you greatly rejoice, though now for a little while you may have had to suffer grief in all kinds of trials. These have come so that the proven genuineness of your faith—of greater worth than gold, which perishes even

though refined by fire—may result in praise, glory and honor when Jesus Christ is revealed. Though you have not seen him, you love him; and even though you do not see him now, you believe in him and are filled with an inexpressible and glorious joy."

SOMETHING TO THINK ABOUT

Today, reflect on a time you felt you should be exempt from a challenge in life.

What made you feel that way?

1. _____
   _____
   _____

2. _____
   _____
   _____

3. _____
   _____
   _____

PRAYER

Father, thank you for helping me to better understand why I am faced with challenges in my life. Thank you for bringing clarity that no one is ever exempt from going through challenges in life. Thank you for making situations easier for me to get through. I know you are by my side and always will be. Please continue to make things work together for my good. Amen.

MY THOUGHTS ON THIS LESSON

JOURNEY SPEAKS

DAY 16
A REFLECTION OF GOD'S LOVE

The only one that can hold the title of being perfect is God. You can strive to be perfect, but you never will be. We will forever be imperfect individuals and that's how God wants things to be. However, you can make decisions to become more like Him. In fact, that is what He wants you do.

God wants you to become more Christ-like and be a reflection of Him, which is the true reflection of who Jesus Christ is. When you become more like Him, you start to notice that your character becomes more like His. The way you conduct yourself reflects Christ's will as well. It's not hard to tell who is and isn't a reflection of God.

Some people you encounter will exemplify that they are followers of Christ before they even open their mouth to tell you. Their actions speak and you can tell by their behavior. There are others who may speak the word of God, but they don't exemplify it in their walk. Even though no one is perfect, you should be able to tell who is on a righteous path without them even mentioning it. God wants us to grow more into the image of His Son Jesus. (Romans 8:29) Going through challenges in life will allow you to get to that point.

Each and every day I wake up with a mindset of being more Christ-like. I ask God to cleanse my heart and make it brand new. Not having a renewed and clean heart makes it impossible to live a changed life. Having a clean heart makes you die to our old-self which is what you want. God will renew your heart if you pray and ask Him.

One way that we can become more like Christ is to love like He does. Loving others may be more natural when it is someone who is part of your family or who you are friends with. But, how are you with loving your neighbor, a complete stranger, or even your enemy?

I know you are thinking how in the world are you supposed to love your enemy. How can you love someone who has hurt you and deceived you? Remember when we talked about forgiveness? Well, that is a way of being able to love them. God still loves you despite your sins, right? Whatever grudge you have with your enemy, let it go. You don't want any of your blessing blocked because of grudges and your inability to forgive.

Loving your enemy is a true challenge. Especially if they used to be a friend or loved one that may have broken your heart or betrayed you. That can be difficult to overcome. You may be left thinking, if a friend would do that to me, who can you trust? But, you cannot be a reflection of God if you can't love your enemies. You should love everyone just as God does us. God is love and His love is to be shown through his people.

God's love is available for us all no matter what we do, good or bad. He will never take His love away from us. No matter who you are or what your background, God loves you unconditionally.

LESSON
Make an effort to love like God loves.

1 Corinthians 13:4-5 NIV

"Love is patient, love is kind. It does not envy, it does not boast, it is not proud. It does not dishonor others, it is not self-seeking, it is not easily angered, it keeps no record of wrongs."

Matthew 5:43-48 NIV

"You have heard that it was said, Love your neighbor and hate your enemy. But I tell you, love your enemies and pray for those who persecute you, that you may be

*children of your Father in heaven.
He causes his sun to rise on the evil
and the good, and sends rain on the
righteous and the unrighteous. If you
love those who love you, what reward
will you get? Are not even the tax
collectors doing that? And if you
greet only your own people, what are
you doing more than others? Do not
even pagans do that? Be perfect,
therefore, as your heavenly Father is
perfect."*

Luke 6:27-31 NIV

*"But to you who are listening I say:
Love your enemies, do good to those
who hate you, bless those who curse
you, pray for those who mistreat you.
If someone slaps you on one cheek,
turn to them the other also. If
someone takes your coat, do not
withhold your shirt from them. Give
to everyone who asks you, and if*

anyone takes what belongs to you, do not demand it back. Do to others as you would have them do to you."

SOMETHING TO THINK ABOUT

Today, reflect on why it's important to love like God loves.

Can you think of some people that you need to forgive?

1. _____
   _____
   _____

2. _____
   _____
   _____

3. _____
   _____
   _____

PRAYER

Father, I thank you for making me imperfect. Thank you for helping me to understand that you are the only perfect one. Help me to become more like you daily. Show me and teach me how. Allow me to continue to have a forgiving heart and forgive others quickly without holding a grudge. Thank you. Amen.

MY THOUGHTS ON THIS LESSON

_____

_____

_____

_____

_____

_____

_____

_____

_____

_____

_____

_____

_____

_____

_____

JOURNEY SPEAKS

Day 17

THE STRENGTH OF GOD

I've come to realization that challenges in life often require a lot of strength that we never knew we had. As I mentioned before, your character is shaped by your strength. You must remain strong to persevere. God will be the one to see you through it all.

I developed strength early in my life by watching my family members. I come from a very strong family, so it's kind of like my strength was an inheritance. We have always prayed together and prayed for one another. Worshiping was always a bonding experience for us. God has blessed many of my close relatives with the ability to fight through and be strong no matter what. With everything that we have been through in our lives we have had to remain strong and trust in God.

I didn't have a choice but to remain strong when I was going through all of the trials and tribulations in my life. Although a couple of times I've thought about giving up, but giving up just wasn't in me. Giving up wasn't an option and even though things were tough I still wanted to keep on going. I sensed that whatever happened to me in life, I would somehow be just fine.

I have always been a fighter and I knew if I kept on pushing, that I would continue to get even stronger. Although they seemed to get more difficult each time, I was able to endure more with each new challenge. Having strength helped me to exercise my endurance and pull through. I was getting stronger both physically and mentally. You have to have tough skin to be able to survive is this world. In fact, looking back over my life, I have realized that my strength has become one of my greatest assets.

LESSON
Strength from God will carry you through.

Psalm 28:7-8 NIV

"The Lord is my strength and my shield, and my heart trusts in Him, and He helps me. My heart leaps for joy, and with my song I praise him. The Lord is the strength of His people, a fortress of salvation for His anointed one."

Habakkuk 3:19 NIV

"The Sovereign Lord is my strength, He makes my feet like the feet of a dear, He enables me to tread on the heights."

Psalm 22:19 NIV

"But you, Lord, do not be far from me. You are my strength; come quickly to help."

Isaiah 40: 29 NIV

"He gives strength to the weary and increases the power of the weak."

Psalm 119:28 NIV

"My soul is weary with sorrow, strength me according to your word."

SOMETHING TO THINK ABOUT

Today, reflect on your level of strength.

How has strength from God carried you through?

1. _____
   _____
   _____

2. _____
   _____
   _____

3. _____
   _____
   _____

PRAYER

Father, thank you for blessing me with your strength. Thank you for making me the strong person that I am. Help me to remain strong through my trials and tribulations. Help me to look to you only when I am weak. Amen.

MY THOUGHTS ON THIS LESSON

_____

_____

_____

_____

_____

_____

_____

_____

_____

_____

_____

_____

_____

_____

JOURNEY SPEAKS

Day 18

KEEP IT MOVING

If you still have breath in your lungs and a beating heart, you have to keep it moving forward in life. God has allowed you to wake up another day for a reason and it was not by accident. Life goes on regardless of what you may be going through. God will see you through no matter what and He is not finished with you yet. You still have a purpose to fulfill. Continuing to push and keep going will become easier with time.

Be proud of yourself when you make strides towards moving forward in your life. Moving forward is challenging and won't be easy. Try not to be so hard on yourself and don't beat yourself up. As you start to move forward you will be able to look back and see how far you have come.

One time in particular that was hard for me to move forward was after the experience of a break up. No one enjoys being hurt and many different emotions took over me. My emotions got the best of me and I was filled with a lot of hurt, pain, frustration, sadness, and loneliness. I had been deceived pretty badly after I had let my guard down and given so much of myself in the relationship.

My intuition kicked in and told me that something wasn't right, so I prayed and asked God to reveal it to me and He did just that. God revealed to me that he was deceiving me and living a double life. God protected me and removed him from my life. God protected me from any other pain and suffering that could've occurred. It's always a good thing for you to pray and ask God to reveal to you the person you are dealing with. Without a doubt He can and will. I do this now beforehand to prevent heart break.

As I moved forward with my life, I reminded myself that things happen for a reason. I prayed and asked God for His strength, healing and guidance in moving forward. I was able to forgive my ex for the pain he caused me and I was successfully able to move on with my life.

Some people in your life will either be a lesson or a blessing. When God removes someone from your life it is for a good reason. Don't try to open doors that He has already closed and don't look back. Whatever God takes away He will bless you with something even better as He did with Job in the Bible.

I reminded myself that God has called me for greater things and in order for me to fulfill my purpose I would need to move forward with my life. I thought it would take me months to get over the relationship, but through prayer and reading God's word, He healed me very quickly. The power of prayer, faith and trusting is real.

LESSON

Don't be afraid to move forward in life.

Revelation 3:7-8 NIV

"To the angel of the church in Philadelphia write: These are the words of him who is holy and true, who holds the key of David. What he opens no one can shut, and what he shuts no one can open. [8] I know your deeds. See, I have placed before you an open door that no one can shut. I know that you have little strength, yet you have kept my word and have not denied my name."

2 Corinthians 5:17 NIV

"Therefore, if anyone is in Christ, the new creation has come: The old has gone, the new is here!"

SOMETHING TO THINK ABOUT

Today, think about a time that you had to move forward in life.

How did God help you to move forward?

1. _____
   _____
   _____

2. _____
   _____
   _____

3. _____
   _____
   _____

PRAYER

Father, thank you for the ability to move forward in life. Thank you for showing me the situations and people that I need to move forward from. Thanks for the covering and protection that you provide me. Please continue to cover me and protect me. Amen.

MY THOUGHTS ON THIS LESSON

_____

_____

_____

_____

_____

_____

_____

_____

_____

_____

_____

_____

_____

JOURNEY SPEAKS

DAY 19
ENJOY THE LITTLE THINGS IN LIFE

As you get older you start to realize that life is more enjoyable when things are simple. Life is too short to live with lots of complexities. Simplicity goes a long way. People have a tendency to make life complicated when it wasn't designed to be that way.

Learn how to enjoy the little things in life and you will start to see a difference. You can start off by making some daily changes in your life to get fulfilling results.

I consider myself to be a person that enjoys the simple things in life. I have learned to prioritize my needs before my wants. Having to find a balance between the two can often times be a struggle. When I am faced with making that decision, I side with the simpler way of doing things over the complicated one.

My Pastor used to preach many sermons on simplicity. His sermons helped me gain a better understanding of living a more simplified life. I started incorporating simplicity and it has definitely proven to decrease the amount of chaos in my life.

Enjoying the simple things in life will make you start to appreciate life more and you will be surprised about how much of a difference it can make.

There are several different ways you can get in the mindset of enjoying the simple things in life. For example, instead of eating out all of the time, you can cook at home. I've actually had some fun experiences trying new recipes. I often try to remake dishes that I've tried at a restaurant. Or have a picnic at the park and invite your friends and family. Having a picnic allows you to enjoy the outdoors in an intimate setting with the people you enjoy the most. You would be surprised at how much fun having a picnic can be. Make an effort to start finding joy and happiness from simple things. Once you get the hang of it, it will get easier and it will become second nature.

LESSON
Simplify your life and enjoy the simple things.

Ecclesiastes 5:18-20 NIV

"This is what I have observed to be good: that it is appropriate for a person to eat, to drink and to find satisfaction in their toilsome

labor under the sun during the few days of life God has given them—for this is their lot. Moreover, when God gives someone wealth and possessions, and the ability to enjoy them, to accept their lot and be happy in their toil—this is a gift of God. They seldom reflect on the days of their life, because God keeps them occupied with gladness of heart."

SOMETHING TO THINK ABOUT

Today, think about how you can exercise simplicity in your life.

What are some things that you can do to live a simpler life?

1. _____
   _____
   _____

2. _____
   _____
   _____

3. _____
   _____
   _____

PRAYER

Father, help me simplify my life. Provide me with the necessary steps to take in order to make this possible. Allow me to be able to enjoy the simple things in life and not take a single day for granted. Amen.

MY THOUGHTS ON THIS LESSON

_____
_____
_____
_____
_____
_____
_____
_____
_____
_____
_____
_____
_____
_____

JOURNEY SPEAKS

Day 20
MISTAKES & SUFFERING

Some challenges and suffering are brought on by our own mistakes. Don't be the type of person that blames God, Satan and everyone else for your mistakes. In life you're going to make mistakes; there is just no way around it. As I've mentioned before, we are imperfect people living in an imperfect world so mistakes are to be expected.

There is a cause and effect for everything. One mistake may cost you your life. Some mistakes can't be prevented, while others can. Make better decisions about things that you allow into your life. Go to God in prayer first and let Him lead you. Hearing a word from God will help you make better decisions. Going to family and friends for advice is not always best. There is nothing wrong with going to them, but make a point to hear from God about the matter first. Taking advice from the wrong people and not being able to distinguish God's voice from that of Satan can cause suffering. Make sure you are slow to listen to God. He will always lead you to make the right decision.

Sometimes people go to other people and things first before God. Don't be afraid to go to Him first because He wants to help you and to meet all of your needs. Talking to family members or friends can give you instant solutions to your problems, however God's answers although they may take a while, are most definitely worth the wait. It takes discipline to go to God first instead of others. You need to be led by God and His word because you need the spiritual interaction with your Father.

LESSON

God will bring you through your challenges even if you have brought them on yourself.

1 Peter 5:10 NIV

"And the God of all grace, who called you to his eternal glory in Christ, after you have suffered a little while, will himself restore you and make you strong, firm and steadfast."

Romans 5:3-4

"Not only so, but we also glory in our sufferings, because we know that suffering produces perseverance"

SOMETHING TO THINK ABOUT

Today, think about a time you brought suffering upon yourself.

How did God bring you through your suffering?

1. _____
   _____
   _____

2. _____
   _____
   _____

3. _____
   _____
   _____

PRAYER

Father, thank you for bringing me through my sufferings, especially, those that I have brought upon myself. Thank you for loving me unconditionally. Please forgive for not obeying your word at times. Please help me to make better judgement and decisions. Amen.

MY THOUGHTS ON THIS LESSON

DAY 21
GOD'S PROTECTION

Challenges in your life sometimes occur because God is protecting you from a bigger problem. You may not see the problem coming, but He does and He will protect you. He knows everything that is going to happen and when it is going to happen as well. Everything is done for His good. Always remember that He is your main source of your protection.

A form of rejection is actually God's protection. For example, don't force different relationships that you know won't work and that God is trying to remove you from. Love yourself more and make some changes in your life. I see many people staying together in relationships that are unhappy. No relationship will be perfect, but you know what you should and should not put up with. Stop getting into relationships just to say you have someone because of loneliness. Pay attention if God is showing you red flags and telling you to remove someone from your life or to dismiss yourself from a relationship. Not only pay attention, but be obedient because He only wants the best for you. If He hasn't shown you, then ask Him to show you and He will. You might be surprised about what He will reveal to you.

The world is filled with an enormous amount of evilness, danger, demons and principalities, so you need God's protection. Pray and ask God to cover you daily because you're going to need it. Before you leave your home each morning, ask Him to cover you and to keep you safe. Pray over your loved ones because they need protection too. Don't ever walk outside without being protected and covered.

One morning on my way to work an eighteen wheeler truck almost hit me. I kept thanking God for protecting me and keeping me out of harm's way. The crazy thing about it is that I didn't even see the truck coming. It's like one minute there was no one in the opposite lane then the next minute there was a truck speeding pass me trying to run me off the road. It was a very scary situation that could have taken my life. I'm grateful that I was under God's protection and covering.

Have you ever experienced anything similar to that? God has protected you more times than you have probably even noticed.

LESSON
God is your protector.

Psalm 121:5-8 NIV

*"The LORD watches over you—
the LORD is your shade at your right
hand; the sun will not harm you by
day, nor the moon by night.
The LORD will keep you from all
harm— he will watch over your life;
the LORD will watch over your
coming and going both now and
forevermore."*

Psalm 32:7 NIV

*"You are my hiding place; you will
protect me from trouble and surround
me with songs of deliverance."*

Exodus 14:14 NIV

*"The LORD will fight for you; you
need only to be still."*

Proverbs 18:10 NIV

"The name of the LORD is a fortified tower; the righteous run to it and are safe."

Psalm 16:8 NIV

"I keep my eyes always on the LORD. With him at my right hand, I will not be shaken."

SOMETHING TO THINK ABOUT

Today, reflect on a time that God protected you from something bad happening.

What did God do to protect you?

1. _____

2. _____

3. _____

PRAYER

***Father, thank you for protecting me and
intervening in my life. I do not know what
could've happen, but you intervened and kept me
safe and sound. Thank you for having the ability
to change the outcome of things. I realize that you
are the only one that can do so. Please continue to
have your hands on me and my loved ones. Amen.***

MY THOUGHTS ON THIS LESSON

_____

_____

_____

_____

_____

_____

_____

_____

_____

_____

_____

_____

_____

_____

_____

_____

_____

JOURNEY SPEAKS

DAY 22
STEP 1 TOWARDS MOVING FORWARD:
EASE YOUR MIND

Whatever you went through most likely took a major toll on you and your life. You need to gather your thoughts and ease your mind as you start to move forward. Easing your mind is one of the keys towards moving forward. Take plenty of deep breaths and exhale as much as you need to. Let anything go that is overwhelming to you and trying to hold you back. Try something new or different.

An excellent way to ease your mind is to get active and start exercising because it makes you feel much better and gives you bursts of energy. Exercising, yoga and meditating are three things that can make you feel great mentally. If you are just starting out, remember to take it easy, because you don't want to overexert yourself.

Try not to be so hard on yourself. Make sure you are not cluttering your mind with too many negative thoughts. Especially, thoughts that seem to keep you up at night. For instance, when it is time for bed, is it hard for you to shut off your thoughts? It is for me at times and I have to remind myself to shut them off and go to sleep. Most of my *bright ideas* come to me at night time which is interesting to me.

Are you like that? Don't let your thoughts keep you up at night because you need your rest. God wants to ease your mind so that you can sleep peacefully. *Sweet dreams!*

LESSON
Take your first step towards moving forward by easing your mind.

1 John 14:27 NIV

"Peace I leave with you; my peace I give you. I do not give to you as the world gives. Do not let your hearts be troubled and do not be afraid."

Philippians 4:7 NIV

"And the peace of God, which transcends all understanding, will guard your hearts and your minds in Christ Jesus."

Numbers 6:24-26 NIV

"The LORD bless you and keep you;
the LORD make his face shine on you
and be gracious to you;
the LORD turn his face toward you
and give you peace."

SOMETHING TO THINK ABOUT

Today, reflect on the importance of easing your mind.

What are some ways that you can ease your mind?

1. _____
   _____
   _____

2. _____
   _____
   _____

3. _____
   _____
   _____

PRAYER

Father, thank you for creating steps to help me move forward. Thank you for creating such a process. Please help me to ease my mind. Show me ways to do so. Help me to get pass the negative thoughts that are holding me back and keeping me up at night. Release anything that is weighing me down. Bring me peace and harmony. I receive it. Amen.

MY THOUGHTS ON THIS LESSON

_____

_____

_____

_____

_____

_____

_____

_____

_____

_____

_____

_____

_____

_____

JOURNEY SPEAKS

DAY 23
STEP 2 TOWARDS MOVING FORWARD:
WRITE DOWN YOUR THOUGHTS

I have always loved writing from early on in my life. When I was little, I would write thoughts in my diary and journal. All throughout school, I used to love writing. My favorite was writing essays and doing book reports. All types of writing would interest me because it was something that I enjoyed. The greatest thing about it is that I always got pretty good grades on my writing assignments.

In my adult years the love for writing carried on. I am the type of person that writes almost everything down. From, grocery store lists, to notes in Church from my Pastor's sermon. I just absolutely love to write and always will.

I often look through my belongings from when I was a child and see different things that I wrote. For me, it's exciting to go back and reflect on the old imes. Recently I found a to-do list in one of my old journals that listed all of my goals and aspirations in life. One of the things on my list was to become and author and write my first book and to get it published. Needless to say my Father in Heaven has answered that for me and what a blessing it is to be able to check that off of my list.

Writing your thoughts down is a great way for you to move forward in life. Keeping a collective journal is a great way to capture your thoughts and to express how you are feeling. Writing your thoughts down can be a tremendous help when overcoming an obstacle in life. When you write your thoughts down, you are setting your mind free from being cluttered.

Journaling allows you to remove things from your head and separate yourself from the impact of the experience that you went through. Having too much on your mind can be very unhealthy and lead to depression and suicide. I suggest that you buy a notebook of some sort, if you don't already have one, and start writing your thoughts in it daily. Journaling is not gender specific and it is also healthy for men too. So, men I want you to also buy a notebook and start writing some things down. It's quite alright if you don't want to call it journaling, I understand. But start to do it and you will see how rewarding and helpful it is. Sometimes men have another style of writing down their thoughts through songs, poems or raps.

You can start off by writing down how you feel, and what is going on with you in your life daily. Some other ideas are to write something you learned new that day or something that you accomplished. Write down whatever you feel led to and make sure you remain consistent with it because that's the key. Within no time you will start to see how helpful getting your thoughts down on paper daily really is.

LESSON

Journaling is an immense way to help in the process of moving forward.

Habakkuk 2:2 NIV

"Then the LORD replied: write down the revelation and make it plain on tablets so that a herald may run with it."

Job 17:9 NIV

"The righteous keep moving forward, and those with clean hands become stronger and stronger."

SOMETHING TO THINK ABOUT

Today, think about how important it is to journal your thoughts.

How can journaling improve your life and help you with moving forward?

1. _____
   _____
   _____

2. _____
   _____
   _____

3. _____
   _____
   _____

PRAYER

Father, I thank you for the ability to write. Thank you for creating my hands and fingers to write with. Help me to feel more comfortable with writing things down. Allow the journaling process to be a great experience for me. Help me to clear my mind daily and be able to rest easy. Thank you. Amen.

MY THOUGHTS ON THIS LESSON

_____
_____
_____
_____
_____
_____
_____
_____
_____
_____
_____
_____
_____
_____
_____
_____

JOURNEY SPEAKS

Day 24
STEP 3 TOWARDS MOVING FORWARD: ESTABLISH A CONNECTION WITH GOD

A significant part of moving forward is spending time with God and reading His word. I know that we live in a busy world with busy lives, but you can find the time. You fit things in your schedule and make time for what you want to make time for. You make daily choices as to what you spend your time doing. Rearrange your schedule and include God in it daily. Start your day by spending much needed time with God and it definitely will improve your day.

Spending time with God brings you closer to Him and strengthens your relationship with Him. He wants to spend time with you daily, so take a few moments in the morning to focus your heart on the truth of His presence with you in every circumstance. Allow His love to guide you through your day and all that you do.

In order to have a closer relationship with God, you have to seek Him diligently. Establish a connection with Him and His presence.

He is longing for you to get closer to Him. He knows how busy you are, but He wants His time and for you to put Him first in your life. He understands exactly what you are going through even when you think He doesn't. Your Father in Heaven knows all of your circumstances and everything that goes on. Leaning on Him is the perfect thing to do in a process of moving forward. The Bible is a book of instruction, filled with information with regards to how you are supposed to live your life. Every answer to questions about life can be found in the Bible. You have to actually pick it up and a read it. Don't go off of what other people say that's in it, take a look for yourself. Start studying what's in the Bible daily. Allow the word inside of you and memorize scriptures to hold onto in your daily walk.

Reading God's word gives you a better understanding as to why things happen in your life. The rewards you receive from reading the word are wisdom, knowledge and power. Reading the word gives you a sense of peace pass all understanding, which comes from Jehovah Shalom who is your "Prince of Peace."

LESSON
Connecting with God through reading His word is a key factor towards moving forward.

Proverbs 8:17 NIV

"I love those who love me, and those who seek me find me."

Deuteronomy 4:29 NIV

"But if from there you seek the Lord your God, you will find him if you seek him with all your heart and with all your soul."

Psalm 63:1 NIV

You, God, are my God, earnestly I seek you: I thirst for you, my whole being longs for you, in a dry and parched land where there is no water.

SOMETHING TO THINK ABOUT

Today, reflect on what spending time with God means to you.

How can you incorporate spending time with Him and reading the Bible daily?

1. _____
   _____
   _____

2. _____
   _____
   _____

3. _____
   _____
   _____

PRAYER

Father, thank you for making it possible for me to have a close relationship with you. Thank you for being my Heavenly Father. I want to be close to you and there's nothing in this world that compares to such greatness. I appreciate the fact that Your word is available to me always. Amen.

MY THOUGHTS ON THIS LESSON

_____

_____

_____

_____

_____

_____

_____

_____

_____

_____

_____

_____

_____

_____

_____

_____

_____

JOURNEY SPEAKS

DAY 25
STEP 4 TOWARDS MOVING FORWARD:
UNDERSTAND THAT YOUR BODY IS A TEMPLE

When you are going through challenges in your life, it is easily to forget about your well-being. For instance, if you are dealing with the loss of a loved one passing, you might not want to eat. Or maybe you are the opposite and start to over eat. Your sleep patterns might also be affected by what you're going through. Your showers or baths might even decrease because you are grieving and still trying to process what has happened.

In the bible it says that your body is a temple of the Holy Spirit and that you glorify God with your body. Which means you have to take care of yourself properly.

Moving forward in the area of self-care is very important because you don't want to let yourself go. Make sure you are still showering daily, doing your hair, brushing your teeth etc. You also may develop a habit of wanting to sleep all day, thinking you can sleep your pain away.

When I lost my children I had trouble sleeping in the beginning. Then, I started spending too much time in the bed and wanting to just - *sleep*. Those were normal reactions, but in the moving forward process, I had to stop doing those things.

I remember my doctor asking me how things were going for me at home. I told him that I was wanting to sleep most of the day away and he encouraged me not to do that. I truly thank him for being honest with me and the fact that he wanted to see me move forward with my life. I prayed and asked God to give me a new outlook on life and to help me to move forward daily with my healing process. I wanted more energy to be better equipped for what God had planned for me.

Reward yourself for taking leaps of faith towards moving forward. It is sometimes uneasy to do, so applaud yourself when you have made even a small stride. Whatever rewarding yourself looks like to you, may be different from others. When I want to reward myself or pamper myself I go to the spa and get a massage to relax. What do you like to do for yourself? *Treat yourself today!*

LESSON
Don't neglect yourself because of a challenge you are going through.

1 Corinthians 6:19-20 NIV

"Do you not know that your bodies are temples of the Holy Spirit, who is in you, whom you have received from God? You are not your own; you were bought at a price. Therefore honor God with your bodies."

1 Corinthians 3:16-17 NIV

"Don't you know that you yourselves are God's temple and that God's Spirit dwells in your midst? If anyone destroys God's temple, God will destroy that person; for God's temple is sacred, and you together are that temple."

SOMETHING TO THINK ABOUT

Today, reflect on the importance of taking good care of yourself.

How can you take better care of yourself during a challenge?

1. _____
   _____
   _____

2. _____
   _____
   _____

3. _____
   _____
   _____

PRAYER

Father, I thank you for your goodness and the ability to move forward. Please show me the areas where I neglect to take care of myself. Help me to not be so hard on myself, though. Give me true joy and happiness that I can only receive from you. Amen.

MY THOUGHTS ON THIS LESSON

_____
_____
_____
_____
_____
_____
_____
_____
_____
_____
_____
_____
_____
_____
_____

JOURNEY SPEAKS

DAY 26
STEP 5 TOWARDS MOVING
FORWARD:
FOCUS ON THE POSITIVE

Because of the type of world we live in, it is often hard to be positive. There is so much negativity around us that we encounter daily. Every direction you look, you see negative things going on.

When it comes to moving forward in your life you have to make a decision to let positivity flow deep within you. Positivity is healthy in moving forward and you can't move forward without it. When you are focusing on negative things, they start to consume you. All forms of negativity hold you back and knocks you off track. Your goal is to stay on track.

It might sound weird, but some researchers say that your brain has a natural inclination to focus on negativity. Release any and everything that has anything to do with negativity. Negativity weighs you down and it is not good for your forward mobility. Positivity uplifts you.

Separate yourself from those that speak negatively. Removing yourself from negative outlets includes people as well. Negative people will bring you down and eventually it will rub off on you. There are people in the world that thrive off negativity and those are the people you want to distance yourself from. However, continue to pray for them. The goal is for you to move forward so get the negative sources out of your life immediately, no matter who they are. If they want to know why you have distanced yourself from them, proudly let them know that you don't have any time for negativity, because you are moving forward in life.

Gather everything that you have learned from your challenge and separate what is positive, and remain focused on that. If you think about it hard enough you will be able to pull some positives out of what you went through. For instance, with the passing of my favorite cousin of cancer, the positive thing is that He is now in Heaven and not suffering anymore.

LESSON

Positivity allows you to move forward, while negativity holds you back.

Proverbs 13:20 NIV

"Walk with the wise and become wise, for a companion of fools suffers harm."

1 Corinthians 15:33 NIV

"Do not be misled: bad company corrupts good character."

Proverbs 22:24 NIV

"Do not make friends with a hot-tempered person, do not associate with one easily angered."

Proverbs 27:17 NIV

"As iron sharpens iron, so one person sharpens another."

SOMETHING TO THINK ABOUT

Today, reflect on your circle of friends.

Do they bring positivity to your life or do they bring negativity?

1. _____
   _____
   _____

2. _____
   _____
   _____

3. _____
   _____
   _____

PRAYER

Father, I thank you for the positives in my challenges. Thank you for the ability to let go of anything that is negative. Please help me to separate the positives from the negatives. Allow me to focus only on what is positive. Block out anything that will try and hold me back. Reveal to me who brings positivity to my life and who brings negativity. Remove anyone from my life who is a negative influence no matter who they are. Provide me with the strength to be able to handle what you reveal to me. Help me to move forward. Amen.

MY THOUGHTS ON THIS LESSON

_____
_____
_____
_____
_____
_____
_____
_____
_____
_____
_____

JOURNEY SPEAKS

DAY 27
LET CHALLENGES ELEVATE YOU

I want you to know that you have the ability to reach the stars. The trials and tribulations that you have gone through made you come out a lot stronger than when you first started. I bet you can get through just about anything now and your level of endurance has increased. I know you can see how much you have grown and developed because of everything you've been through. *Think back for a moment.*

Believe in yourself and know that you can set goals and accomplish them. Never let anyone tell you anything different. You must believe in yourself and be your own biggest fan. Support from others is great, but don't rely on it because sometimes people may disappoint you. They may not give you the encouragement that you feel you deserve.

One thing to remember is that it doesn't mean that someone isn't happy for you just because they didn't offer you the support that you want from them. People may support you in their own way. To be honest; they might not know how to provide good support so don't rely on it. Honestly you can't always expect someone to have the same passion for something as you do. Just appreciate whatever support is provided to you. Pick your battles and don't get mad about it and hold a grudge. Lean on God and allow Him to be your biggest supporter because He will never disappoint you. Pray and ask Him to place people in your life who will support you genuinely.

You can do just about anything that you put your mind to it. The sky is the limit; but you have to put in the work. Know that you are on your way to greatness, so elevate your mind to *think big*. You can accomplish all of your dreams and goals in life.

When you *think big*, you also begin to *dream big* and *bigger things* are the outcome. Stay consistent with your goals by writing them down and having a plan of action to accomplish them.

LESSON
Challenges in life help you reach the stars. The sky is the limit!

2 Chronicles 15:7 NIV

But as for you, be strong and do not give up, for your work will be rewarded."

Psalm 37:4-5 NIV

"Take delight in the LORD, and he will give you the desires of your heart. Commit your way to the LORD; trust in him and he will do this."

Isaiah 32:8 NIV

"But the noble make noble plans, and by noble deeds they stand."

SOMETHING TO THINK ABOUT

Today, set some short and long terms goals for yourself.

What are some ways you can accomplish your goals?

1. _____
   _____
   _____

2. _____
   _____
   _____

3. _____
   _____
   _____

PRAYER

Father, thank you for elevation. Thank you for the ability to reach a higher capacity. Help me to dream big. Please allow me to accomplish every goal that You set for me to achieve. Help me to align my life with Your word. Help me to believe in myself. Amen.

MY THOUGHTS ON THIS LESSON

JOURNEY SPEAKS

Chapter 28
MAKING A CONSCIENCE DECISION TO MOVE FORWARD

Moving forward is a part of life. Making a decision to move forward starts in your mind first. If you feel you can move forward, then you will be able to do so. If you feel stuck, and can't move forward, then ask God to help you move forward and to show you where to start. Go to Him in prayer and talk to Him about your thoughts. Tell Him exactly how you are feeling and what your concerns are. You have to trust in Him and know that He will show you what to do. Let Him guide you and help you in the process of moving forward. It is going to take some hard work and effort on your part, but allow Him to lead you. Dedication and determination are two important factors that play a tremendous role in the process of moving forward.

Starting the process of moving forward made me feel good because I knew that I had my Heavenly Father by my side. I knew things would get better eventually, but I didn't know how long it would take. I was able to smile again because I had made a decision to take a leap of faith and knew something good would be the outcome. When God has His hands in a situation the outcome is always good.

LESSON
Making a decision to move forward starts in your mind.

Deuteronomy 1:6 NIV

"The LORD our God said to us at Horeb, "You have stayed long enough at this mountain."

Isaiah 43:18 NIV

"Forget the former things; do not dwell on the past."

Psalm 34:4 NIV

"I sought the LORD, and he answered me; He delivered me from all my fears."

SOMETHING TO THINK ABOUT

Today, pray and ask God to help you to move forward.

What are some things He revealed to you in moving forward?

1. _____
   _____
   _____

2. _____
   _____
   _____

3. _____
   _____
   _____

PRAYER

Father, thank you for dedication. I know that dedication isn't easy, so thank you for helping me to put forth the effort to move forward. Please help me to continue to put my trust in you. I know that you will see me through. Amen.

MY THOUGHTS ON THIS LESSON

_____

_____

_____

_____

_____

_____

_____

_____

_____

_____

DAY 29
YOUR CHALLENGES CAN HELP OTHERS

Don't ever think that you are the only one going through a particular challenge in life. Even though those around you might not be going through your same exact situation, there is someone in the world that is. There is someone who can relate to you and your situation.

There are help groups in your area that provide support. All you have to do is go online and do a search of the particular help group that you are looking for. For instance, when I was going through the loss of my children, I felt no one understood. I searched online for a group of women who had also suffered the loss of children. The program consisted of mentors who would reach out to you via email to share stories and have a line of communication. It helped and it was great to have someone to talk to. But, my main source of healing came from God because I continued to trust Him through my pain.

I have made it a point to comfort other women who have also been through the same struggles as I have. Going through trials alone is not easy and can lead to major depression. I have been a listening ear and have helped many women through their healing process. We have fed off of each other's strength, prayed for one another and kept an open line of communication.

Even if you have never been through what someone else is going through, you should still offer your comfort. It doesn't take a degree to know how to lend thoughtful words of encouragement to others. People are committing suicide daily because they don't have a support system. You could be the one to help save someone's life. You never know what people are going through and they could be *suffering in silence.*

If you know someone is going through a difficult time, take a few minutes out of your day to check on them. A quick text message, email, or phone call, goes a long way. Let them know you are thinking about them and that you care. Don't just tell them that you will pray for them, actually pray for them. You want prayers when you are going through something, so make sure you are genuinely praying for others. Pray for God to give them peace, strength, and the ability to move forward in their life.

LESSON

Through your experiences, you can help others.

Galatians 6:2 NIV

"Carry each other's burdens, and in this way you will fulfill the law of Christ."

1 Thessalonians 5:11 NIV

"Therefore encourage one another and build each other up, just as in fact you are doing."

Proverbs 3:27 NIV

Do not withhold good from those to whom it is due, when it is in your power to act.

SOMETHING TO THINK ABOUT

Today, reflect on how your experiences can help others.

What are some ways that your experiences can help them?

1. _____
   _____
   _____

2. _____
   _____
   _____

3. _____
   _____
   _____

PRAYER

Father, thank you for my experiences. Thank you for bringing me through each and every one of them. Please allow me to be of assistance to others when I can, who are going through challenges I have been through. I know You have put me through these experiences for a reason. Provide others with comfort the way you have comforted me. Amen.

MY THOUGHTS ON THIS LESSON

_____

_____

_____

_____

_____

_____

_____

_____

_____

_____

_____

_____

_____

_____

_____

_____

_____

DAY 30
SHARE YOUR TESTIMONY

Every person in the world is unique and has a unique story to tell. As you have learned throughout my book, your challenges in life shape your character and help you to grow. The trials that you go through, don't last forever. God removes you out of darkness and into His marvelous light.

Trials are an opportunity for you to share a great testimony with others. Give your testimony as often as you can give it. Giving your testimony lets everyone know that you are giving God all of the glory He deserves.

Testify and let people know how good He is and how He has delivered you. Declare that you are still standing strong, having faith and trusting in your Heavenly Father with your whole heart. We are supposed to honor the Lord by bearing witness to others about how He has worked in our lives.

Share your story with others. It's not always about being secretive and not wanting others to know what you have been through. By telling your story you can help numbers of people. More people than you actually think need to hear *your* story. Thousands or even millions of people can be impacted by *your* story. Think about how many people's stories have impacted you. Not just people on television or the radio, but people all around you.

Your story or experience could be what someone needs to hear. Others could be ready to give up on life, until they hear *your* testimony. Be a positive influence in other people's lives. There are people doing great works for the kingdom, but there is always a need for more. There could never be enough positivity in the world, so if you have not already, start making *your* contribution today.

I share my testimonies every single chance that I can. I used to feel ashamed and embarrassed about sharing my testimony because of what other people would think. I don't feel that anyway anymore because God wants me to share my story and continue to bring glory to His Holy name. I made it through all of my challenges that I faced in my life because of Him. As a Father He helped me to forgive those who hurt me, helped me remain strong, taught me discipline, covered and protected me, filled my voids and most of all healed me.

The things that He helped me through and delivered me from, He can also do the same for you. Life is too short not to experience the goodness that He has to offer you, so don't waste another minute without it.

LESSON

Challenges leave you with an amazing testimony to share with others.

Psalm 66:16 NIV

Come and hear, all you who fear God; let me tell you what he has done for me.

Psalm 71:14-17 NIV

As for me, I will always have hope; I will praise you more and more. My mouth will tell of your righteous deeds, of your saving acts all day long—
though I know not how to relate them all. I will come and proclaim your mighty acts, Sovereign Lord; I will proclaim your righteous deeds, yours alone. Since my youth, God, you have

taught me, and to this day I declare your marvelous deeds."

Revelation 12:11 NIV

They triumphed over him
by the blood of the Lamb
and by the word of their testimony;
they did not love their lives so much
as to shrink from death.

Mark 5:19 NIV

Jesus did not let him, but said, "Go home to your own people and tell them how much the Lord has done for you, and how he has had mercy on you."

SOMETHING TO THINK ABOUT

Today, reflect on your testimony and what God has done for you in your life.

How can your testimony help someone today?

1. _____
   _____
   _____

2. _____
   _____
   _____

3. _____
   _____
   _____

PRAYER

Father, thank you for bringing me out of what I thought was darkness. Challenges in life are brought on me for a good reason. Thank you for showing me that life's challenges happen for a reason and that You will always help me through them. Thank you for my testimony and helping me to share it and to bring all the glory to your name. Amen.

MY THOUGHTS ON THIS LESSON

_____
_____
_____
_____
_____
_____
_____
_____
_____
_____
_____
_____
_____
_____
_____
_____
_____
_____

JOURNEY SPEAKS

SOURCES

New International Version (NIV)
Holy Bible, New International Version®, NIV®
Copyright ©1973, 1978, 1984, 2011 by Biblica,
Inc.® Used by permission. All rights reserved
worldwide.

ABOUT THE AUTHOR

Journey Speaks has been known as "the strong and courageous one," for quite some time because of her strength and courage. No matter her struggle, trial or tribulations, being a strong woman of God has allowed her to consistently move forward in life. She found God very young which has helped her to keep things together. Through everything she says, "my Lord & Savior Jesus Christ has kept me in His light. No matter what happens, I know He is with me."

She has always had a strong passion for writing which began when she was only five years old.

Reflecting on 1Corinthians 16:14 which says, "Let All You Do Be Done In Love", led to her start a ministry offering the opportunity to help those in need, and to volunteer to feed and clothe the homeless and less fortunate.

Another passion of hers is being a part of the children's ministry at church in which she is able to teach the children about God and His love for us all. Each child holds a very special place in her heart.

In everything that she does, she wants to express her love to others from now until eternity as God does for all of us!

FOR BOOKING:

WEBSITE:
IAMJOURNEYSPEAKS.COM

FACEBOOK:
AUTHOR JOURNEY SPEAKS

INSTAGRAM:
@IAMJOURNEYSPEAKS

PLEASE CONTACT US FOR ALL PUBLIC SPEAKING ENGAGEMENTS, PRESS, AND ANY OTHER PUBLICITY INQUIRIES.

Thank you!

Made in the USA
Columbia, SC
19 July 2018